A New School
for Megan

Story by Jenny Giles
Illustrations by Rachel Tonkin

2

Zoe and Kylie looked up
as Mr. Jackson, the principal,
came into their classroom
with a new girl.
She still had her backpack on,
and she looked very shy and scared.

"Good morning, everyone,"
said Mr. Jackson. "This is Megan,
and she's going to be in your class.
She has just moved here,
and she hasn't had time
to make any friends yet."

Zoe looked over at Kylie.
"Megan can come and sit with us,
Miss Bell," she said.

"And we'll show her
where everything is," said Kylie.

"Thank you, girls," smiled Miss Bell.
"That is very kind of you."

Megan was very quiet all morning.
She sat between Zoe and Kylie,
and they helped her with her work.

When it was time to play outside,
the three girls
walked around together.

There were children everywhere...
running and laughing and shouting.
Megan stayed close to Zoe and Kylie,
and she jumped whenever
one of the children ran past her.

They went for a walk to the fort,
but too many children were playing there.
Kylie asked Megan
what she wanted to do,
but Megan didn't answer her.
She just stood and stared
at all the children
on the playground.

Kylie and Zoe didn't know
what to do next.

Then, over on the other side
of the playground, they noticed
some of the children from their class
playing four square.

"Let's go and play four square,"
said Zoe.
"Do you want to come, Megan?"

Megan still didn't answer,
but she nodded.

"Come on, then," said Kylie.
"Let's go and have a game."

The girls waited in line
and watched the game.

"You have to hit the ball
into one of the other squares,"
Luke said to Megan.

"And if you miss it, or hit it
over the line, you're out," said Kylie.
"It's your turn now. Go on."

Megan went and stood
in the empty square.

Zoe and Kylie talked to each other
as Megan began to play.
"Megan hasn't said anything all day!"
said Kylie.
"Do you think she can talk?"

"I don't know," said Zoe,
"but she doesn't seem very happy,
does she?"

"She doesn't seem to like our school,"
said Kylie, "and she doesn't seem
to like us, either."

Then Luke shouted,
"Hey! Look at Megan."

Zoe and Kylie looked up.

13

Megan was hitting the ball
every time it came to her!

Zoe and Kylie watched in surprise
as she won the next game.
All the children in the line
had their turn, but no one
could score against Megan.

Everyone cheered and clapped,
and Megan started to smile
for the first time that day.
Mr. Jackson came over to watch.
"Well done, Megan!"
he called.
"It looks as if you are
having a good day at our school."

"Oh, yes, Mr. Jackson!" said Megan.
"Zoe and Kylie are my friends,
and four square has always been
my favorite game.
Now I'm **glad** I came to this school!"